MW00892778

HOW TO TRAIN YOUR AUSTRALIAN SHEPHERD :

Expert tips and techniques for raising a happy and well-behaved Aussie

Dr. Robert Riddle

All right reserved. No part of this publication may be reproduced, distributed, or transmitted in any form or by any means, including photocopying, recording, or other electronic or mechanical methods, without the prior written permission of the publisher, except in the case of brief of quotations embodied in critical reviews and certain other noncommercial uses permitted by copyright law. Copyright © Dr. Robert Riddle, 2023.

Table of contents

Introduction to Australian shepherd puppies

Aussie Puppy History

The Australian Shepherd, commonly known as the "Aussie," is a herding breed of dog that originated in the Western United States, not Australia as its name suggests. The breed was developed in the 19th century by Basque shepherds who emigrated from Europe to the western United States, particularly California. The Basque shepherds brought with them their dogs, which were known for their exceptional herding and guarding abilities.

These dogs were bred with local breeds in the United States, including the Collie and Border Collie, to create a new breed that could handle the tough conditions of the American West. The breed was further developed during the 20th century by ranchers and farmers who continued to breed the dogs for their herding and working abilities.

Despite their name, Australian Shepherds did not originate in Australia. The breed received its name from the fact that some Australian Shepherds were imported to Australia from the United States to work on ranches and farms. The breed became popular in Australia, and many Australians began breeding them. The name "Australian Shepherd" was given to these dogs to reflect their Australian heritage.

The breed gained recognition by the American Kennel Club (AKC) in 1991 and has since become a popular breed in the United States and around the world. Today, Australian Shepherds are used for a variety of tasks, including herding, search and rescue, therapy work, and as family pets.

Australian Shepherd puppies are born with a variety of coat colors, including black, blue merle, red, and red merle. Their coats can be either straight or wavy and require regular brushing to prevent matting and tangling.

Overall, the Australian Shepherd has a rich history as a working breed that has adapted to life in the American West. Its intelligence, loyalty, and high energy make it a popular breed for those who enjoy outdoor activities and need a companion who can keep up with their active lifestyle.

Characteristics of the breed

Australian shepherd puppies are a medium-sized breed that typically weighs between 35 and 65 pounds and stands 18 to 23 inches tall at the shoulder. They have a dense double coat that can be black, blue merle, red, or red merle, and they often have distinctive white markings on their face, chest, and legs.

In addition to their striking appearance, Australian shepherd puppies are known for their intelligence, athleticism, and loyalty. They are highly trainable and excel in a variety of dog sports, including agility, obedience, and herding competitions. They are also known for their affectionate and loyal nature, making them excellent family pets.

Temperament and behavior

Australian shepherd puppies are active, energetic dogs that require plenty of exercises and mental stimulation. They have a high prey drive and may chase small animals or children if not properly trained and socialized. They are also known to be vocal and may bark or whine if they are bored or not getting enough attention.

With proper training and socialization, however, Australian shepherd puppies can be excellent companions. They are highly trainable and eager to please and can learn a wide range of commands and tricks. They are also affectionate and loyal to their owners and can form strong bonds with their human families.

Importance of training for Australian Shepherd puppies

Because of their high energy levels and intelligence, Australian shepherd puppies require plenty of training and socialization to thrive. Without proper training, they may become bored, destructive, and difficult to manage. They may also develop behavior problems, such as anxiety, aggression, or separation anxiety.

Training can also help Australian shepherd puppies develop the skills they need to excel in dog sports and other activities. For example, obedience training can help them learn basic commands, such as sit, stay, and come, which are essential for safety and control. Agility training can help them develop the coordination, speed, and agility they need to compete in agility competitions.

Overall, training is essential for Australian shepherd puppies to develop into well-behaved, well-adjusted adult dogs. It can help them build strong bonds with their owners, develop their cognitive and physical abilities, and prevent behavior problems.

Chapter 1: Preparing for training

Preparing for training is an essential step in ensuring the success of your Australian shepherd puppy's training program. This involves understanding your puppy's needs, setting up a safe and comfortable environment, and selecting appropriate training tools.

Understanding your puppy's needs

Before you begin training your Australian shepherd puppy, it's important to understand their needs. Australian shepherd puppies need a consistent routine and clear rules and boundaries to feel secure and well-adjusted.

To meet your puppy's needs, you should establish a daily routine that includes regular exercise and training sessions. You should also provide plenty of mental stimulation, such as puzzle toys, interactive games, and training exercises. Finally, you should establish clear rules and boundaries for your puppy, and be consistent in enforcing them.

Creating a safe and comfortable environment

Creating a safe and comfortable environment is essential for your Australian Shepherd puppy's training program. You should provide a secure, designated area for your puppy to sleep, eat, and play, such as a crate or playpen. You should also ensure that your home is puppy-proofed, with hazardous items and areas inaccessible to your puppy.

In addition, you should provide plenty of toys, treats, and comfortable bedding for your puppy. This will help them feel secure and happy, and encourage them to learn and engage in training exercises.

Selecting appropriate training tools

Selecting appropriate training tools is important for ensuring that your Australian shepherd puppy's training is effective and humane. You should choose tools that are appropriate for your puppy's age, temperament, and training goals.

Common training tools for Australian shepherd puppies include:

Treats: Treats are a valuable tool for positive reinforcement training. You can use small, soft, and smelly treats to reward good behavior and encourage your puppy to learn new commands.

Clicker: A clicker is a small handheld device that makes a clicking sound when pressed. You can use a clicker to mark the moment your puppy performs a desired behavior, and then reward them with a treat.

Leash and collar: A leash and collar are essential for teaching your puppy to walk on a leash and for keeping them safe during training exercises.

Training treats pouch: A training treat pouch is a small bag or container that you can attach to your waist or belt. It allows you to keep treats handy and easily accessible during training sessions.

Interactive toys: Interactive toys, such as puzzle toys or Kongs filled with treats, can provide mental stimulation and help prevent boredom during training breaks.

By selecting appropriate training tools, you can make your Australian Shepherd puppy's training program more effective, enjoyable, and humane.

Basic training commands

Basic training commands are essential for teaching your Australian shepherd puppy to behave well and respond to your commands. These commands lay the foundation for more advanced training exercises and can help you establish a strong bond with your puppy.

Sit:

The "sit" command is one of the most basic and important commands you can teach your Australian shepherd puppy. It's easy to teach and can be used in a variety of situations, such as when greeting visitors or during mealtimes.

To teach your puppy to sit, follow these steps:

Hold a treat close to your puppy's nose, then move it slowly upwards and backward towards their ears. As you do this, your puppy will naturally sit down to keep their balance.

As soon as your puppy sits, say "sit" and give them the treat.

Repeat this exercise several times, gradually using the "sit" command before your puppy sits down.

Once your puppy is consistently sitting on command, gradually phase out the use of treats, using praise and affection instead.

Stay:

The "stay" command is another important command for teaching your Australian shepherd puppy self-control and obedience. It can also be a useful safety command, preventing your puppy from running into dangerous situations.

To teach your puppy to stay, follow these steps: Begin by commanding your puppy to "sit".

Once your puppy is sitting, hold your hand out in front of you, with your palm facing your puppy, and say "Stay".

Take a step backward, while still facing your puppy, and wait a few seconds.
If your puppy remains sitting, return to them and give them a treat and praise.
Gradually increase the distance and duration of the "stay" command, always returning to your puppy to reward them for their good behavior.

Come:
The "come" command is an essential safety command for ensuring that your Australian

shepherd puppy comes to you when called. It can also be useful for controlling your puppy's behavior in public places.

To teach your puppy to come, follow these steps: Begin by calling your puppy's name in a friendly, happy tone of voice.
As your puppy approaches you, say "Come" and reward them with a treat and praise.

Repeat this exercise several times, gradually increasing the distance between you and your puppy.
Once your puppy is consistently coming when called, you can begin to phase out the use of treats, using praise and affection instead.

Down:
The "down" command is another important basic command for teaching your Australian shepherd puppy obedience and self-control. It can also be useful for calming your puppy in stressful or exciting situations.

To teach your puppy to lie down, follow these steps:

Begin by commanding your puppy to "sit".

Hold a treat in front of your puppy's nose, then move it slowly towards the ground, saying "down" as you do so.

As your puppy follows the treat, their body will naturally lie down.

As soon as your puppy is lying down, give them the treat and praise them.

Repeat this exercise several times, gradually using the "down" command before your puppy lies down.

Once your puppy is consistently lying down on command, gradually phase out the use of treats, using praise and affection instead.

Teaching "Leave it" to Australian Shepherd Puppies:

Teaching an Australian Shepherd puppy to "leave it" is a crucial aspect of their training. It involves teaching your puppy to resist the urge to investigate or pick up items on the ground or in their environment that are potentially dangerous or harmful. By teaching them this skill, you can prevent them from ingesting harmful substances, eating garbage, or becoming overly fixated on an object, animal, or person.

Here are some comprehensive steps to follow when teaching your Australian Shepherd puppy to "leave it":

Start with a treat: The first step in teaching your puppy to "leave it" is, to begin with a treat. Hold a treat in your hand and present it to your puppy, but don't allow them to take it. As soon as they begin to show interest in the treat, say "leave it" firmly and then cover the treat with your hand.

Wait for compliance: Wait for your puppy to back off and stop trying to get the treat. As soon as they do, praise them with a "good dog!" and then give them a different treat that you have in your other hand.

Repeat the process: Repeat the process several times until your puppy begins to understand the connection between the "leave it" command and the reward that follows.

Introduce distractions: Once your puppy understands the "leave it" command with a treat, begin to introduce distractions. Place a toy or another item of interest in front of your puppy and use the "leave it" command. When they back away, reward them with praise and a treat.

Increase the difficulty: As your puppy becomes more adept at "leaving it," gradually increase the difficulty of the distraction. This might include adding a food item, a ball, or a person or animal to the mix.

Practice regularly: It is important to practice the "leave it" command regularly to reinforce the behavior. This can be done during walks, playtime, or training sessions.

Use positive reinforcement: Always use positive reinforcement when teaching your puppy to "leave it." Praise and reward them for good behavior, and avoid using physical punishment or negative reinforcement.

By teaching your Australian shepherd puppy these basic training commands, you can help them become well-behaved, obedient, and responsive to your commands. These commands will also form the foundation for more advanced training exercises and activities.

Chapter 2: Training Your Australian Shepherd to Use a Crate

Do you fear your Australian Shepherd will detest his crate?

It requires patience, so go gently through each phase to make sure your puppy has a pleasant training experience.

The following will help you get started:

1. Determine Your Australian Shepherd's Crate Size

Buying a crate that will be the right size for your Australian Shepherd is the first step to success.

How can you tell which size will suit your dog the best? They need to be able to stand up and turn around in it. If the box is too large, It gives them tacit permission to relieve themselves in a remote area of the crate without having to deal with the mess.

If you already have an Australian Shepherd puppy, choose a crate that will fit them when they are fully grown.

2. Introduce your Puppy to the crate slowly.

This is a crucial stage in getting your dog used to the crate. Never go too quickly since it might make your Australian Shepherd feel compelled and ruin the experience.

Put the crate in a space you use often, such as your family room or home office. This allows your dog to adjust to the sight of it there, and he could even start exploring the crate on his own. If not, you may start introducing the crate gradually.

Approach the box while joking with your Australian shepherd dog. To entice your dog to accompany you on the trip, drop a few tasty snacks next to the crate's entrance.

Once this is accomplished, move the goodies so that your Australian Shepherd must stick his head inside the crate to get them. You will advance to throwing goodies to the rear of the crate eventually.

If your dog isn't motivated by food, you may try putting their favorite toy in the cage.

3. Make your Australian Shepherd comfortable.

Additionally, this is an excellent opportunity to ensure that your dog will feel at ease in the crate. If your dog is already housebroken, you may be able to line the bottom of the crate with a dog bed or a towel. If your dog is likely to destroy it or urinate on it, you should refrain from doing this. If your Australian Shepherd is now unable to securely have anything comfy in their box, don't feel awful. You may introduce it at a later time.

4. Start kenneling your Australian shepherd with rewards.

The process of kennel training your dog may now begin in earnest.

Give your dog a command, call them over to the crate, and then signal them to go in with your hands. Never force them into the crate. Use food to entice them into the crate if necessary. Give them the food reward once they are safely in the crate, then gently close the door. For the first few times, when they are in the crate, stay close to your Australian Shepherd. Before releasing them, spend five to ten minutes sitting calmly next to them.

You may start to leave the room after a few repetitions of practicing in this manner. Keep the practice sessions brief and repeat them numerous times throughout the day. Work your way up to leaving them in the crate for extended periods until you can do so comfortably for around 30 minutes.

5. Lengthen the Crate's Stay

You may begin leaving your Australian Shepherd in his crate while you are away after he is used to doing so for a full thirty minutes while you are home.

This is a fantastic time to begin associating good things with their crate since they will be in it for extended amounts of time. Give them a favorite toy instead of a reward once they enter.

A Kong ball that has been filled with cream cheese or peanut butter is popular among dogs. Even overnight storage in the freezer will help the meal last longer for them. This offers your dog something to anticipate when you leave and distracts them from thinking about being in the crate.

Keep in mind that your Australian Shepherd is still not used to spending the whole day in a crate. They need some kind of physical activity every few hours, or at the absolute least, a restroom break.

A puppy that is being trained to use a crate cannot hold onto its bladder for more than three to four hours. Make sure your dog has enough restroom breaks to set him up for success.

Be careful not to become too excited when you go back to let your dog out. Both your dog and his owner will be delighted to see each other.

However, if you overexcite them each time you come home, you could make them more nervous. Keep your entrance somber and composed.

6. Sleeping in a Crate

You are now prepared to attempt to get your Australian Shepherd to sleep in the crate. Keep the crate nearby when you are sleeping. It should ideally be in your bedroom with you.

This enables you to hear whether your Australian Shepherd puppy has to go potty in the early morning. It implies that mature dogs who are just learning to use a crate won't feel as lonely and uneasy when they sleep. Because he is a sociable animal, your dog will always want to be as near to you as possible.

Use the same command you typically use to get your Australian Shepherd inside the box. As always, follow it up with a treat. Your dog can start whining at first throughout the night.

Try your best to ignore this even though it might be bothersome while you are trying to get some quality rest. Your Australian Shepherd is probably only screaming for attention. Don't give their complaints any kind of consideration, either favorable or negative.

This may also be a good time to think about adding a blanket to the box or using a somewhat darker crate, such as a flight kennel. This lessens the amount of visual stimulation your dog is exposed to and may hasten their ability to relax.

Chapter 3: Australian Shepherd Potty Training

Australian Shepherd puppy training is a crucial element of dog ownership. To prevent accidents in the home and to preserve your puppy's health and well-being, you must educate them on where and when to relieve themselves. To properly potty train your Australian Shepherd puppy, follow these detailed steps:

Establish a schedule

Setting up a schedule is the first step in potty training your Australian Shepherd puppy. Puppies need a regimen to learn when to feed, play, and relieve themselves. Make sure your puppy has a regular feeding schedule and go outdoors often throughout the day. You may remove them right away in the morning, after meals, and just before night.

Select a Location

Decide where in your yard you want your dog to relieve himself. They will be able to locate the area in the future thanks to the aroma of their pee and waste. Make sure the location is convenient and offers space for your puppy to roam about.

Use a Command

Decide on a particular command that you will use each time your puppy needs to go pee outdoors. For instance, you may say "Go potty" or "do your business." Your dog will learn to connect the command with the activity if you use the same command each time.

Watch Your Puppy

Keep an eye on your puppy at all times, particularly in the beginning while toilet training is being done. Put your dog in a crate or an area with puppy pads when you can't watch them to prevent accidents.

Praise and Reward

When your puppy uses the specified toilet area, reward them by giving them goodies or vocal praise. Your dog will repeat the activity with encouragement from a positive reward.

Accidents will always occur during toilet training, therefore it's important to deal with them properly. Say "no" firmly and take your puppy out to the appropriate area as soon as you catch them in the process of pottying inside. Use an enzymatic cleanser to properly wipe up the dirt and get rid of any scents that could tempt your dog to relieve itself there again.

31

Be persistent

Teaching a puppy to use the toilet requires persistency. Keep your schedule, orders, and incentives constant. Although they may make errors, your puppy will eventually figure out where and when to relieve themselves.

Lastly, it takes time, persistence, and positive reinforcement to toilet-train an Australian Shepherd puppy. Create a schedule, choose a location, give a command, keep an eye on your puppy, praise and treat them, deal with accidents correctly, and be patient. Your puppy will eventually learn where and when to use the restroom, and you will have a happy and healthy companion as a result.

Chapter 4: How to train your Australian Shepherd puppy to walk on a leash

Every dog should be able to walk on a leash. It not only enables them to go with you, their favorite person, but it also ensures their safety (as well as the safety of other dogs and humans). No matter if you like the calm rural life or the metropolis, your dog should always be walked on a leash. It takes time to train them to walk with you, but with persistence and encouragement, you and your dog will soon be taking regular walks together.

How to Get Your Dog to Enjoy Leash Walking

1. Introduce Markers

A marker, also known as a bridging stimulus, is a spoken cue or physical cue that indicates when your dog performed an action that earned them a reinforcer (a reward). A fantastic example of a marker (and conditioned reinforcer) is a clicker. You may use a consistent word, such as "yes" or "good," or a hand gesture, like a thumbs up if you don't have a clicker. Pick one, however, and stay with it. As soon as you see the behavior, note it. Your ability to mark gets more effective the faster and more precisely you can.

2. Establish a Positive Network

Your dog has to be at ease and appreciate wearing walking gear before you take him on an outside outing. His collar, leash, and maybe a body harness are included in this. Make sure you are in a peaceful, unobtrusive section of your house, such as the living room. Give your dog some time to get accustomed to wearing each item at first. While he plays inside or goes outside to use the restroom, put his collar on, marking and reinforcing each time by rewarding your dog. For brief periods throughout the day, fasten the leash to the collar. Be careful to note and reward him each time he takes a few steps while wearing it. If you're going to use a body harness, ease him into it by rewarding him as you put it on over his head and fasten the straps.

3. Train Your Aussie to Pay Attention

While it would appear as if you should immediately start walking with your dog, you need to be sure he is genuinely paying attention before you go since else, he could pull and dart about. Wait patiently for even a fleeting glance or instant of eye contact from your dog before marking and reinforcing the behavior. Repeat this often to help your dog learn that staring at you is rewarded with rewards. A "cue" for attention may also be added. Right before your dog is going to glance at you, say "look" or "eyes," and then mark, reinforce, and reward.

4. Back up and begin to move

This may seem counterintuitive, but it works wonders. Simply take a few steps backward while your dog is on a leash, and reward him as he follows. Gradually increase the number of steps you take backward, while still encouraging your furry friend to stay close by your side.

5. Exercise using come

By teaching your dog to come to you on command, you'll avoid any future issues with pulling or rushing during walks. Start by tossing a treat a short distance away from you, while your pup is on a leash. Then, call out "Come" and reward him as soon as he turns to face you. Keep repeating this process until it becomes a fun game for your furry friend.

6.Practice taking a few steps with your leash outside

You may start moving outdoors after your dog has learned the fundamentals of leash training inside, but be sure to choose a location with minimal distractions. You should consider using your garage or backyard. Practice taking a short distance before stopping and calling for help. Every few steps (while moving), mark and praise instances of good leash walking, and once you stop, wait for their attention before rewarding them as well. Do not hurry! Baby steps in every direction.

7. Increase Distance Gradually

Move out of your house and into the neighborhood gradually. Start by just walking one or two houses, and as your dog becomes better, gradually increase the distance. As your dog masters this set of abilities, make sure to consistently praise and note his progress. It takes work to become proficient at synchronizing the delivery of the mark and treat while moving, but after a few days of practice, you will be an expert. Keep going and be optimistic!

Though they appear to have boundless amounts of energy, keep in mind that puppies have short attention spans. A young dog won't be able to go large distances with you until they are older and more mature. Allow your dog to smell, do a little doggy emailing on shrubs and trees, and just enjoy being outdoors with you. Walkies should never be a duty or an opportunity to do a flawless heel.

Chapter 5: Socialization

Socialization is an important aspect of training for Australian shepherd puppies. It involves exposing them to different people, animals, and environments, so they can learn how to interact with the world around them. Socialization is crucial for the mental and emotional well-being of your puppy and helps them become a well-adjusted and confident adult dog. Here are some tips for socializing your Australian Shepherd puppy:

Introduce Your Puppy to Different People

Introduce your puppy to a variety of people, including men, women, children, and people with different ethnic backgrounds, clothing, and appearances. This will help your puppy become comfortable around different people and learn how to interact with them. Here are some tips for introducing your puppy to people:

Start with familiar people, such as family and friends, and gradually introduce your puppy to new people.
Encourage people to approach your puppy in a friendly and non-threatening manner.
Reward your puppy with treats and praise when they interact with people calmly and positively.

Introduce Your Puppy to Different Animals

Introduce your puppy to other animals, such as dogs, cats, and small animals, so they can learn how to interact with them. This will help your puppy become comfortable around other animals and reduce the risk of aggressive behavior towards them. Here are some tips for introducing your puppy to animals:

Start with well-behaved animals and gradually introduce your puppy to new animals.
Monitor your puppy's behavior closely and intervene if necessary.

Reward your puppy with treats and praise when they interact with other animals calmly and positively.

Expose Your Puppy to Different Environments

Expose your puppy to different environments, such as parks, beaches, and busy streets, so they can learn how to adapt to new surroundings. This will help your puppy become confident and comfortable in new environments and reduce the risk of fear and anxiety. Here are some tips for exposing your puppy to different environments:
Start with quiet and familiar environments and gradually expose your puppy to more challenging environments.
Keep your Australian shepherd puppy on a leash and under control all the time.

Reward your puppy with treats and praise when they handle new environments calmly and positively.

Be Patient and Consistent

Socialization takes time and patience, and it's important to be consistent and persistent in your efforts. Here are some tips:

Take small steps and don't overwhelm your puppy with too much too soon.

Practice socialization regularly, ideally every day. Be patient and positive, even if your puppy is initially fearful or anxious.

By following these tips, you can help ensure that your Australian Shepherd puppy becomes a well-adjusted and confident adult dog. Socialization should be done positively and consistently, using positive reinforcement and avoiding punishment or harsh corrections.

Chapter 6: Exercise and Physical Activity

Australian shepherd puppies are energetic and active dogs that require regular exercise and physical activity to stay healthy and happy. Lack of exercise can lead to behavioral problems such as excessive barking, destructive chewing, and aggression. Here are some tips for providing your Australian shepherd puppy with enough exercise and physical activity:

1.Daily Walks

Take your puppy for daily walks to provide them with the necessary exercise and physical activity. Australian shepherd puppies need at least 30-60 minutes of exercise per day, depending on their age and energy level. Regular walks can also help reduce anxiety and improve socialization skills.

2.Interactive Playtime

Interactive playtime is a great way to provide your puppy with both exercise and mental stimulation. Use toys such as balls, frisbees, and ropes to engage your puppy in games such as fetch and tug-of-war. This can also help increase and strengthen the bond between you and your puppy.

3.Agility Training

Agility training is an excellent way to engage and challenge Australian shepherd puppies physically and mentally. As a high-energy and intelligent breed, Australian shepherds thrive on activities that require quick thinking and physical stamina. Agility training offers a great opportunity to bond with your puppy while providing them with a healthy outlet for their energy.

Here are some tips for agility training your Australian shepherd puppy:

Start with basic obedience training:
Before introducing your puppy to agility obstacles, ensure they have basic obedience training. Commands such as sit, stay, come, and heel are essential for safety and control during agility training.

Gradually introduce agility equipment:
Start with simple obstacles such as tunnels, weave poles, and jumps. Allow your puppy to explore the equipment at their own pace and reward them for successful attempts.

Positive reinforcement:
Australian shepherd breeds respond well to positive reinforcement training. Use treats, toys,

and verbal praise to motivate your puppy to complete the agility course successfully.

Practicing regularly:
Consistency is really important when it comes to agility training. Practice regularly, even if it's just for a few minutes each day, to help your puppy build confidence and muscle memory.

Keep it fun:
Agility training should be enjoyable for both you and your puppy. Make it a game, and use a happy tone of voice to keep your puppy engaged and enthusiastic.

Consult with a professional:
Consider enrolling your puppy in a formal agility training program or working with a professional trainer. They can guide equipment selection, course design, and proper technique, as well as help you identify areas where your puppy needs improvement.

Prioritize safety:

Always prioritize your puppy's safety during agility training. Ensure they are physically ready for the challenges of agility, and that equipment is properly set up and secured. If you notice any signs of pain or discomfort, stop the training and consult with a veterinarian.

Agility training can be a fun and rewarding activity for Australian shepherd puppies. By following these tips and prioritizing safety and positive reinforcement, you can help your puppy build confidence, improve their physical abilities, and strengthen your bond with them.

5. Swimming

Swimming is another great form of exercise for Australian shepherd puppies. It's a low-impact activity that can help improve cardiovascular health and build muscle strength. However, not all Australian shepherd puppies are natural swimmers, so it's important to introduce them to water gradually and provide them with a life jacket if necessary.

6. Mentral Stimulation

6. Mental Stimulation

Australian shepherd puppies are highly intelligent and require mental stimulation as well as physical exercise. You can provide mental stimulation by teaching your puppy new tricks, playing hide-and-seek, or using puzzle toys that require problem-solving skills.

7. Consistency and Safety

It's important to provide your Australian Shepherd puppy with consistent exercise and physical activity. This means sticking to a routine and ensuring that your puppy gets enough exercise every day. It's also important to ensure that your puppy is safe during exercise and physical activity. This means providing them with a secure leash and collar, avoiding extreme weather conditions, and keeping them away from dangerous or harmful objects.

By providing your Australian shepherd puppy with enough exercise and physical activity, you can help ensure that they remain healthy, happy, and well-behaved. Exercise should be tailored to your puppy's age and energy level, and should always be done safely and consistently. Remember to also provide your puppy with mental stimulation, such as training and puzzle toys, to keep them mentally engaged and stimulated.

Conclusion

Training an Australian Shepherd puppy can be a rewarding and fulfilling experience for both the owner and the dog. These intelligent and energetic dogs thrive on positive reinforcement and consistent training. By establishing a strong bond with your puppy, setting clear boundaries, and providing plenty of mental and physical stimulation, you can help your Australian Shepherd puppy reach their full potential.

Remember that training is a lifelong process, and your Australian Shepherd will continue to learn and grow throughout their life. With patience, consistency, and a positive attitude, you can build a strong relationship with your furry companion and enjoy the many joys that come with having a well-trained Australian Shepherd by your side. So, get started with training your Australian Shepherd puppy today, and have fun watching them grow into a happy, well-behaved adult dog.

Made in the USA
Monee, IL
27 August 2024

64649482R00031